Rainbows After The Storm

When someone you love
becomes a memory, then the
memory becomes a treasure

By

Sherry Boyd Neu

Tate Publishing, LLC

"Rainbows After the Storm" by Sherry Boyd Neu

Published in the United States of America
by Tate Publishing, LLC
127 East Trade Center Terrace
Mustang, OK 73064
(888) 361–9473

ISBN: 1–5988629–2-8

Endorsements

The book is excellent! Something that will benefit others who have to endure this existence of living without their child–their heart. Also, those who have not experienced this pain can get a glimpse of the darkness and despair and be able to reach out to grieving parents in a better way.

-Ben's mom-Kathy

None of this would have occurred except for the Storm that was and will always be a part of Sherry's life. And to think that in her death, Stormie ultimately was the tool that gave her mother life. She was in tune with a higher power and God has used that in many ways–ways that will be unknown and others well known as time goes by. Stormie was born to be an angel and returned to her angelic form when her time came. We will never as humans understand that. As a mother, I can only imagine how devastating it can be.

-Ruby Cruise

Grief is a process. It is a process that some cultures understand, welcome and support, and a process that other cultures, such as our own, fear and avoid. But the truth about grief is that the only way *out* of it is *through* it. It takes a particular kind of courage to face grief head on and dive into its teachings. This courage is what Sherry Neu chose to find. This book provides a rare glimpse into the Rite of Passage that grief truly is. Sherry has found a beautiful—and often beautifully simple—way to share what it is to be taught, to be moved, and to move through, grief. All grief is devastating. The grief from the loss of a child is a particular flavor of hell. It is a suffering that every parent fears. We imagine that we would die if this brand of suffering were to visit our home. But Sherry did not die. She found the courage and love in herself, in her God, and for her daughter, to be changed, transformed, and ultimately reborn into a new person through this caldron of feelings. We cannot turn off our pain without also turning off our joy. Sherry describes in this book how to have them both.

This book gives some insight, some beams from a distant light house, to guide each of us to the possibilities of surviving our own grief, and to assist us in supporting those people we know, whether in our own family, at work, or in our community, who are in this grief journey. Knowing what not to say, and more importantly, what *to* say, can make the difference between our avoiding those who are grieving, and our being able to support them in their journey. This is a travel guide of sorts; through a land we hope not to have to visit. But in truth, we all experience grief in our lives. We all can use a guidebook through that foreign land. Sherry's poignant, painful, funny and insightful book is a rare message back from the crucible of loss, to encourage the rest of us to choose to *live,* even in the face of death. I know Stormie is proud of her Little Mama.

-Arianna Gray, M.A.-Counselor

Dedications

Jesus for my many blessings

My precious only child . . .
Stormie Lynn Schott
May 7, 1977—March 11, 2001
I loved you first and your leaving first breaks my heart. Nothing on earth can separate us . . . Not time, not space . . . not even death!"

Mother and Daddy; I love you so!
"Keep Smiling"

My sister-friends.

The unconditional love of my husband, Timothy.
He stands in front of me to protect me,
Beside me to walk with me,
And behind me to catch me.

Table of Contents

Foreword

When I met Sherry Boyd Neu, she was a student entering a business school to upgrade her professional skills. As a single mother, she was not only interested in earning a higher salary, but showing her daughter the importance of continuing your education.

Sherry had just recovered from a debilitating back injury and subsequent surgery and needed new skills to return to work. When I discussed the entry salaries for graduates of our school she told me that was not enough money and indicated that she would do much better than the average. I loved her moxie and belief in herself.

Sherry not only graduated, but entered a job making much more than the average graduate; in fact the school hired her to teach other women re-entering the work force. Her enthusiasm, compassion and natural teaching abilities were an asset to our staff.

As my friendship with Sherry grew, I enjoyed watching Sherry's daughter Stormie grow into a beautiful and confident young woman full of grace. Stormie excelled in everything she attempted and entered college with many wonderful experiences under her belt. Her strong religious faith was shown not only by her actions, but also by the many Christian missions she attended as a young girl and later as an undergraduate and graduate student.

Her pride in her Mome (Stormie's name for Sherry) and her step-father Tim Neu was apparent in her actions, comments, and the wonderful jokes they shared. Sherry loves to tell stories about Stormie and Tim's ongoing jokes and pranks they pulled on each other.

My friendship with Sherry has grown into a sisterhood over the last several years. Sherry was instrumental in helping me cope with a life-threatening medical diagnosis and a period where my self-esteem was very low. Her encouragement, love and friendship helped me to get through some very difficult times.

Five years ago when Stormie was involved in a fatal car accident, my friend fell into a deep well of despair from her broken heart. The only way you may ever know how Sherry really felt is to have loved and lost someone so important in your life. Sherry is quick to tell you she hopes you will NEVER know what she has been through after walking through the doors of Hell in that hospital in Waco, Texas.

We have shared tears, friendships with other families who have lost children, and simply spent quiet time together. As circumstance would have it, we have in fact been blessed to spend lots of time together in the last five years. Our personal visits, telephone calls, and e-mail communications are frequent.

It has been wonderful to watch Sherry just begin to emerge from that broken-hearted woman into someone who now smiles again, has begun to write and be artistically creative again. Oh, this wasn't easy for her, in fact she forced herself to face her grief head on in order to heal emotionally so she could help other grieving people. Her honesty, faith, and strong love are apparent in this book.

This book is intended to help you recover from your grief or to help a friend or family member when he or she is grieving. Hopefully you will be able to follow Sherry's lead and see past your broken heart and see the rainbow through your tears. Listen carefully and you may hear angel wings.

-Debbie Coates

Introduction

"I tell you the truth, you will weep and mourn while the world rejoices. You will grieve, but your grief will turn to joy." (John 16:20)

I won't lie to you. I promise you no quick easy remedies. Learning how to live a different life takes a lot of will power and strength. When you lose part of your very soul, your child, there is no rhyme or reason. I don't believe God took my only child. I choose to believe He was there with open arms to cushion her sudden death.

I won't lie to you and tell you that time passing will take the loneliness and suffering away. I know until the day that I hold her in my arms again and smell her special smell I will mourn my loss.

I will promise you there is hope. I will promise you can learn to live the different life that is ahead of you if you choose to. I will promise you can learn how to relocate your grief. I will promise you can find joy again.

"So with you: Now is your time of grief, but I will see you again and you will rejoice, and no one will take away your joy." (John 16:22)

I will promise you if you listen to my journey, and find even a few ideas that make sense, then you have hope to survive. If you find some knowledge and comfort in my healing journey, then my experiences have not gone in vain.

Society has a difficult time in dealing with death. The death of a child evokes such mixed emotions. A parent is not "suppose" to bury their child. Many people said inappropriate words they thought to be comforting.

Don't let anyone fool you; it is a very difficult road to travel. It is hard to concentrate when you are going through grief. I received gifts of books on grief in the early days of my loss, but they were hard to read, long, small print and for lack of better words, sugar coated. Someone who had walked in my shoes did not write them. These are the words and thoughts of a grieving mother. These are my experiences, raw and factual.

I won't lie to you, but I will promise you may have traveled in the stormy doors to a living hell, but through God's promises, you can travel out the doors to rainbow hope.

Words of encouragement . . .

"When the door of happiness closes, another opens, but often times, we look so long at the closed door that we don't see the one, which has been opened for us."

~Helen Keller

I Am Her Mother

"A mother's love for her child is like nothing else in the world. It knows that no law, no pity; it dares all things and crushes down remorselessly all that stands in its path."
~Agatha Christie

My precious Stormie:

You will always walk with me, even though the gates have closed behind you.

I cannot touch your earthly flesh, but you are a living presence with me forever.

You are the . . .

Whisper of the leaves as I walk through our pasture, the blue bird as it hops from limb to limb, the butterfly as it kisses the flowers, the cool hand on my brow when I'm not feeling well.

You live on inside my laughter, and you are crystallized in every teardrop. I am the place your life grew, where you came from, your first home. I was the map you followed with every step your young life took.

I loved you first and your leaving first breaks my heart, nothing on earth can separate us . . . Not time, not space . . . not even death!"

May you catch heaven's rays,
Love you with all my heart, MoMe

I loved her first. My Stormie grew inside me and her movement reminded me of a butterfly fluttering. We both cried together on the day of her birth. I cried without her on the day she died. She was my precious Storm. I would like to tell you I named her Stormie because there was a terrible storm on the day she was born. But the sun shone brightly that day. Maybe in hindsight she was named for the horrific storms that took place on the day of her death and the day of her burial.

I was 22 years old when she was born and we spent the next 23 years growing up together. The responsibilities of caring for a human being were so scary that I almost talked myself out of getting pregnant. My Storm was often called the mother and me the child. She was an old soul in a young person's body. We were one and the same, but upon her death I found she had so many other sides to her that were unknown to me.

I measured my life's worth in being Stormie's mom. No words can describe the depths of my shattered soul when my precious gift returned to her maker. She was killed in an automobile accident while traveling from Houston, TX, where she was visiting her fiancé's parents, back to Waco, TX, where she attended Baylor University. Her death was sudden. No forewarning, nothing. One moment she was alive and the next she was ripped out of my life. She had been engaged a mere nine days. My heart has been shattered into a million tiny pieces, and my soul has wept blood tears until it is numb. I can't begin to understand what God has in store.

I will forever cherish the sweet memories of the last time I went to Waco to visit Storm. We were piled up in the middle of the bed having one of our Mom/Storm talks, when I asked her why she felt such a great desire to travel to foreign countries to spread God's word–why not here in the states where she would be safer?

You see, I always had this overpowering fear of losing her. She told me that God's word was easily heard here, but there were those in other countries that had never heard His name spoken. We each spoke from the heart as we shared our feelings; my greatest gift to God was giving her life, and her greatest gift was spreading His word.

She was getting her masters in political science. She made such an impact at the university that Baylor set up a Stormie Schott Outstanding Student Award that will be awarded yearly to the student that most embodies her beliefs.

How can anybody understand that a vital part of me died with her? I have a great big empty hole in my soul with no purpose left in my life.

But most important, no matter what, *I am her mother.*

Words of encouragement . . .

Real mothers know that a child's growth is
not measured by height or years or grade . . .
it is marked by the progression of Mama to
MoMe to Mom.

Ask My Mama How Is She

My Mama, she tells a lot of lies

She never did before.
From now until the day she dies,
She'll tell a whole lot more.

She used to tell the truth, a lot.
But now it doesn't matter.
I died and went to heaven,
Her life is all a-shatter.
Ask my Mama how is she.
She'll say, "Yes, I'm fine!"
She wants to beg, "Please help me.
I can't find that Storm of mine!"

Ask my Mama, how is she,
She'll say, "I'm alright."
If that's the truth then tell me,
Why does she cry each night?

Ask my Mama, how is she,
She seems to cope so well.
She didn't have a choice, you see,
Nor the strength to yell.

You think you know the feeling,
But this cannot be.
For even though you loved me,
You didn't love as much as she.

She will smile and tell you,
"It's o.k. God has a plan."
But then she'll turn away and cry,
'Cause she just can't understand.

Tell a joke and she will laugh,
But she is not o.k.
She wants to share the joke with me,
But it will not be today.

I watch from here, in Heaven.
Her distress disturbs my peace.
Will someone please take care of her,
And thus take care of me?

"Some day you will feel better."
"Yes I will." she lies.
She knows this will not happen,
Until the day she dies.

"I was so lucky!

I had her all those years!"
They passed in a minute,
I shed so many tears.

Ask my Mama how is she,
She'll say, "Thank you. Good."
She cannot tell you how she feels.
Oh, how I wish she could.

Ask my Mama how is she,
"I'm fine, I'm well, I'm coping."
For God's sake, Mama,
Just tell the truth
Just say your heart is broken.

Ask my Mama how is she,
"I'm well, I'm good. And you?"
I'll shake my head in Heaven.
It simply isn't true.

She'll love me all her life.
I loved her all of mine.
But if you ask how is she,
She'll lie and say she's fine.

Her carnival is over.

She's stepped off the carousel.
But, to save you feeling badly,
She'll say, "Thanks, all is well."

My Mama, she's not gone mad, yet.
But, oh so very nearly.
Don't ask my Mama how is she,
Ask how is she, really.

I am here in Heaven.
I cannot hug from here.
If she lies to you, don't listen.
Hug her, hold her near.

On the day we meet again,
We'll smile and I'll be bold.
I'll say, "You're lucky to get in here, Mama,
With all the lies you told!"
~Unknown

The First Seven Days Of The Death

Call it a mother's intuition; I knew she would not live.

My soul screamed out loud from the moment I received the call Stormie was in an accident. An 18-wheeler hit her small SUV in a rainstorm.

Day of the Death

DESPAIR
When you first get the news–complete heart wrenching sick to your stomach disbelief.

PANIC
Get me to my child now, hurry, hurry, hurry.

DISBELIEF
This can't be happening. Please let it be a mistake. This is a nightmare and I will wake up and my world will be the same.

HELPLESSNESS
It is difficult to accept that we cannot fix our child. The pain cannot be taken away or eased.

FINALITY
The doctor's voice telling you that your child is dead. You are asked if you want to see the body.

LOST
Where do I go? What do I do now? Why do I continue to breathe and she doesn't. How do I live now?

RESPONSIBLITIES
Making phone calls, spreading the news. Making arrangements.

RAW GRIEF
I can't do anymore. I can't function. I can't stand.

I wasn't feeling well the evening of her death. My husband Tim and I weren't home when the call came. We returned to find a message from Stormie's fiancé's father. I almost didn't call because by then I was feeling really sick. When I heard his voice tell me that Storm had been in a serious car accident and was at the hospital, my legs gave out and I crumbled to the floor. I instantly felt her spirit surround me. I knew she would not live. It kept running through my mind that she had gotten engaged just nine days prior and I hadn't seen her engagement ring on her finger.

All the heavens stormed, crying huge tears, which pounded our windshield from the moment Tim and I left our home in Denton to make the 2-hour trip to Waco, TX where she was hospitalized. We left with just the clothes on our backs. All we could think of was get there *now.*

As we traveled down the highway, I called everyone I could think of to pray for her. I called her father, who was also traveling to Waco. We divorced when she was 4 years old. I told him he had to get there quickly because she couldn't die alone. He thought I was crazy telling him she was going to die. He kept telling me she was okay. Tim kept telling me whatever was wrong with her could be fixed. I couldn't convince anyone that she was going to die. I prayed for God to keep her whole. Either take her or leave her here, whatever His will, but keep her body whole.

We were met in the hospital parking lot by several of her friends and guided to a very small "family" waiting room. It seemed liked an eternity but in reality I think we waited about 45 minutes. Then the door to hell opened and in walked two doctors. The voice said that her heart just got tired and quit. I remember falling to the floor screaming out her name over and over and over again, begging her not to leave me behind.

It took me a long time to come to terms that no part of her human body could be harvested. It puzzled me that not even her skin could be used. My mother reminded me of my prayer to God to keep her whole. He honored my prayer.

O God, I have lost so much. Who will fill these gaping holes within me?

The Second Day

GET DRESSED

Comb your hair, brush your teeth, mechanical actions we do everyday of our lives. It takes so much energy.

At the birth of the next morning–the first day of the rest of our lives–we searched for an open store to buy toiletries. We mourned out loud while we gathered toothbrushes, toothpaste, and a hairbrush. People in the store never asked if they could help; they dodged us completely. We needed to be gently guided.

FUNERAL ARRANGEMENTS

Numbly you get in a car and drive to the funeral home. Why is it called a home? You are directed to a private room where a person sits at the head of the table and one of the first questions asked is how are you going to pay for this. You must decide on what music to play, who is going to speak, where the services are going to be held, flowers, and the worst was picking out the box that will forever hold your child's body. What is she going to wear?

Just think, Stormie was engaged just nine days prior to her death. How do you switch from wedding plans to funeral arrangements?

She died out of town. We had to address how to get her back home. More issues were added to an already difficult situation with Stormie's father and I being divorced. Up until two weeks prior to her death, he and I did not speak. When her fiancé, Scott, asked for her hand in marriage, we (being her father, step-mother, step-dad and I) agreed to do everything we could to make this time in her life the happiest. Her father wanted funeral services to be at his church in a town that was different from where I lived. I wanted her to be buried at the cemetery that adjoins my property, my parents' homestead. I needed her close to me.

HOME

Entering the house for the first time–an empty house. It felt so hollow. Even though Stormie was away at college part of the year, she came home at random times. Her room remained as she left it when she drove out the drive to college the first year.

Tim and I had to make the 2-hour journey from Waco back to our home in Denton. Some friends came to Waco to drive us home, but we needed to be together. Security. We had to be able to see, hear, feel, and touch each other to know we weren't alone. Their kindness will never be forgotten.

The Third Day

VIEWING

Who thought up the term *viewing?* Your loved ones' shell is placed in a box and flowers are put around it.

She attended college for five years in Waco. Many acquaintances were made there and a *viewing* and memorial service was requested. I could not *view* my daughter dead. Once again Tim and I made the 2-hour trip back to Waco. We couldn't bring ourselves to go to the funeral home immediately so we just drove around aimlessly.

Allow me to regress for a few moments. Storm was 11-years-old when Tim came into our lives. He took us to a carnival in town and he and Storm rode the Zipper. She panicked and wanted off. A few years later Tim received a letter and picture from Stormie. The picture was of her standing next to a Zipper at a carnival in Waco. The letter said she would rather forfeit the Texas Lottery than ride the Zipper again. She had such a sense of humor. She often gave Tim gifts of CD's and the last one he received was of the country artist Tim McGraw and the title song was Remember Me. Tim and Stormie shared such a strong love.

Now, back to Tim and I driving around Waco. We had no clue where we were driving and it didn't really matter as long as we could avoid the inevitable. We came across a parking lot with a carnival. It was the same location where the picture was taken that Stormie sent to Tim in 1997. At the same exact moment we saw the Zipper, the song Remember Me came on the radio. Tim and I both burst out crying.

Yes, our little girl, we will always remember you!

Words of encouragement . . .

My angel girl whispered a secret to me -
"Whenever you feel a breeze on your face . . .
It's me blowing you angel kisses.
Surrounding you in unconditional love."

MEMORIALS

Time, a matter of seconds, minutes, an hour–a whole person's life can be memorialized.

Some 500 people attended: fellow students, church family, state representative, professors, a homeless man, a cafeteria worker and her 5th grade teacher from Denton. I had no clue she touched so many lives. My only child had many mothers, fathers, brothers and sisters in the name of Christ. I remember walking into the church and seeing the memorial booklet of her services. I eagerly picked one up. It was the first time I saw her birth date and the date of her death together; it took my breath away. I couldn't take the heartbreak and I wept uncontrollably. The trip back to Denton was an eternity.

The Fourth Day

FUNERAL DAY

What do you wear to your child's funeral? What difference does it make?

Once again storms raged and the heavens joined us in our tears. The rainstorm was so intense it was almost impossible to drive to the funeral. A group of Stormie's friends pieced together a video of her and played it at the funeral. My eyes were so cloudy with tears I couldn't see a thing. I remember hearing my child's voice calling to me, laughing, "This snow angel is for you mom." Four years later I got the courage to watch the video.

During the funeral I had this overpowering need to touch her hair. She would always lay her head in my lap and I would run my fingers through her hair. While she was small, I would draw her close to me and reach down to her small head to touch her hair. As she outgrew me, we would hug and I would reach up to run my fingers through her hair. I tried to ignore my need to once again touch her hair. If I touched her hair, I would have to see her body in the casket. My need overpowered my fears and the casket was pulled out of the hearse, and opened up so I could touch her hair, while all the time the rain kept pounding. It felt *bittersweet.* I would never run my fingers through her brown hair again. Her cross necklace was taken from her neck and placed around mine.

Words of encouragement . . .

Faith is not knowing what the future holds,
But knowing who holds the future.

The Fifth Day

Tim and I were completely, totally lost. We almost didn't know how to take a breath. What were we suppose to do now? How were we supposed to live?

It's common for people to do all the *right* things in the very beginning–for instance, attend the funeral, send flowers, and bring food to the family gathering.

After the day of the funeral, nobody brought food. I never before knew the great importance of taking food to the family. I'm sure some asked if they could do something, but my mind wasn't working clearly; and I most likely declined. I wished they had just knocked on the door. I came home once to find the house had been cleaned—such a thoughtful gesture from my mama friend.

Most never called. It was as though they were thinking the funeral was over, they had paid their respects, and it was time to move on as though *it* never happened. Well, let me enlighten you, *it* did happen, and we are *forever* changed.

Words of encouragement . . .

A heart that feels another's pain
Is often blessed with the power to heal it.

The Sixth And Seventh Day

The sixth and seventh days all were a blur. Days didn't matter anymore. Time didn't matter. All we knew was we had to hold on tight to one another or we couldn't survive. I'd always heard the expression to die of a broken heart. Well, there is no doubt in my mind that I would have died from my broken heart had it not been for the fact that I couldn't bear to put my husband, mom and dad through any more pain.

When a child loses a parent he is an orphan.
When a man loses his wife he is a widower.
When a woman loses her husband she is widow.
There is no name for a parent that loses a child,
for there are no words to describe the pain.

When you lose a parent, you lose your past.
When you lose a spouse, you lose your present.
When you lose a child, you lose your future.
~Unknown

How do you choose what to write on the headstone?

She guided me; letter from my journaling
April 6, 2001.

I received a letter from your dad telling me what he, Lark and Scott wanted on your headstone. They are the same verses that Scott chose for the memorial booklet. I didn't want to use the same verses because my mind went immediately to the day of the viewing and the fresh pain from losing you resurfaced. The verse does not bring me peace or a smile to my heart.

Around 9 pm last night I went to your room and started looking at your shelves and the collection you have there. I began crying and praying for you to show me what to do. I do not want to disagree with your father anymore. One of the greatest joys we brought to you was sitting down as a unit when Scott asked us for your hand in marriage. I don't want to take that away from you.

I kept praying, searching and crying until you brought me to a small green journal dated 1995–1996. It was filled with your writings from conferences, Bible studies, Dudley, Touchstone, etc. I found exactly what should go on your headstone. Thank you so much for guiding me to the information.

I called your dad this morning and before I could tell him what I wanted he started apologizing for past wrongs and told me I could put whatever I wanted on your headstone. He told me he, too, was going through your room at his house last night at the same time I was in Denton. He found so many wonderful writings that you had left behind and he shared your great love for me.

He, Lark, Tim and I are meeting this Sunday at Roselawn Cemetery to decide on a headstone and verse. I pray you too will be there to guide us. I love you and miss you almost more than my soul can take.

Some of her journal words written January 29, 1996 are carved into her gravestones.

"For when I feel homesick for Heaven:

'For me, to live is Christ and to die is gain.'
(Philippians 1:21)

The clock of my life is ticking. What do I want my end to be? For Jesus to say, 'Well done, my good and faithful servant.'

Here lies Stormie Schott. One who was faithful, loved those in her care, and showed Jesus through her smile and heart that we now cannot easily forget. She laid her life down so that her God's life might be seen through her. She was not selfish, but joyfully gave all that she had and most of all-herself."

No words can better describe her life!

Words of encouragement . . .

"Yesterday is a dream, tomorrow but a vision.
But today well-lived makes every yesterday
a dream of happiness, and every tomorrow a
vision of hope. Look well,
therefore to this day."
~Sanskrit Proverb

Death Certificate

A death certificate must accompany
all legal documents.

I tried very hard *not* to read her name and cause of death on that horrible piece of paper titled Death Certificate. It says she died from blunt force injuries. Really? Now, if an 18-wheel truck going 60 mph hit your vehicle on the driver's side, I think you would have blunt force injuries. The doctors told me she died on the operating table. Her human body may have died there, but I know her spirit left her body at the time of the accident because it held me as I was told the news of her accident.

Words of encouragement . . .

"The joy one feels, the mourning another
feels in the same world on the same day;
it's a rainbow across the world, many colors
together for such an awesome creation."
~Ruby Cruse

Surviving Stormie's Death

Words of encouragement . . .

Things may seem hopeless right now,
But always remember-
Every colorful rainbow that ever shone came
after the storm.

My pain was raw. It was as if Jesus knew it was more than I could bear. My mind shut down, mentally taking me to a place where I could survive. He allowed me to stay in a state of numbness for days, weeks, months, actually years. I would keep myself together in public, but when I got into my vehicle to drive home, I would grieve out loud. When I arrived home, I would lay my head on the steering wheel and have a big melt down. My dear husband would come and guide me into the house where our dog Mattie met us.

Timothy and I avoided family gatherings. We hated being around *anyone's* family. We felt so out of place. It caused hurt feelings. I tried to explain why it cut so deep in our souls; we had only one child and now our house felt empty. It hurt seeing what they still had and what we didn't. Never again would we have our child or hope for grandchildren. Hectic environments added to our already nervous state of mind. Our future was suddenly ripped out of our lives. Some accepted the explanation, but others couldn't accept our actions. As parents, so much of our lives revolve around our children. How were we going to go on? We were just trying to keep our heads above water.

The greatest gift from this tragedy is my husband and I have grown even closer. We are always good about insisting on talking when one is upset. It's how we have kept ourselves going after our daughter's death.

Words of encouragement . . .

Stop telling God how big your storm is . . .
Instead, tell the storm how big your God is!

Thoughts

Words of encouragement . . .

"The walls we build around us to keep out the sadness also keep out the joy."
~Jim Rohn

Our minds can be the darkroom in which negatives can develop. Thoughts can be very disturbing. Some of mine are below. You may have experienced some of them yourself.

~ I don't like her being dead. I want her here with me suffering.

~ This sucks, it really sucks.

~ I want to die. I made a suicide plan. To go home I must cross a railroad track; to go to the cemetery, I must cross a railroad track. My faith does not allow me to commit suicide, so I just wouldn't look when I crossed the tracks. I reasoned if a train just happened to hit me, then it would be an accident, all my pain would be gone and I would get to hold my baby girl again. Irrational thinking.

~ I hate this life. What will ever be right again? Nothing will ever be the same. We have to learn to live a different life.

~ How am I supposed to pick the real estate to lay her body!

~ Shopping for coffins. What one would fit her personality best? How in God's name do you do that and keep your sanity?

~ I hate seeing the bare dirt that covers her coffin. I see no life, just death.

~ I can't stand the thought of her being in a morgue. It haunts me to imagine my child's body treated that way.

~ Did she feel a lot of pain? Her blood was everywhere. Her fiancé Scott was in the vehicle in front of her. She was following him from Houston back to Waco. He saw the accident and went back. He held her until the ambulance came. He kept telling me that her beautiful face was not injured. My heart goes out to him. I can only imagine what her body looked like. No, please mind, don't go there.

Words of encouragement . . .

When you think your faith has failed you,
All your hopes and dreams are gone,
Listen for the Angel voice
That whispers, "Just hold on."

Things I Did

I found keeping all my grief, emotions, sorrow, anger–everything that you can't even identify and don't need to try–kept me depressed for several years. You may be able to sympathize with some of the things I did.

~ Held tight to my husband, Timothy.
(Now and always)

~ Pulled the covers over my head and refused to get out of bed. (Fourth year)

~ Gazed at nothing at all with a totally blank mind for hours. (Years one-four)

~ Wasn't able to complete a sentence or a thought.
(First moment-fourth year)

~ Closed myself in the closet and sat in the corner weeping until my husband pulled me out.
(Fourth year)

~ Crawled into my husband's lap like a child and crying or just sitting there being held tightly. (Forever)

~ Screamed her name, and that if she loved me, she would not have left me all alone. (Forever)

~ Didn't listen to music at all for long periods of time. (Years one-four)

~ Soaked my pillow with tears, wrung it out and cried some more. (Forever)

~ Found myself at the cemetery, kneeling over her headstone, sobbing uncontrollably, and mourning out loud. (Forever) I actually met 3 different mothers whose children were buried close to mine. I have never met the mother whose daughter is buried the closest; when I take flowers to Stormie, I leave one at her daughter's grave and vice versa.

~ Carried her blood-spattered wallet. (Year one)

~ Inside her wallet I found a card that I had given Stormie when she left for college; I treasure it and it now has a home in my wallet. (Forever) God gives us what we need the most at just the right time. She needed it first, and I need it now.

When you get a case of loneliness and you think nobody's there to love, support, and listen, or to show they even care. Just reach into your pocket and pull out this little card. Nothing could be easier when life seems really hard. And every time you read it, it will help remind you, too, a very special part of me is always there with you.

~ Held on to special items such as her green journal and carried them with me. (Year One)

~ Began sewing quilts to focus my mind on a task. (End of first year-present)

~ Returned to work the following week so I would have to keep moving.

~ Reached out to other mothers who were walking in my shoes. (Forever)

~ My mother and father became even dearer to me. (Forever)

~ Set up my sewing room in her bedroom. I left everything she had on the walls and on her shelves, moved out her bed and computer table and set up sewing. It brings me great comfort being in the surroundings that she chose. (Forever)

~ Began working in the yard–planting flowers, hand-watering foliage, watching the wildlife. (Third year)

~ Painted different rooms in the house. (Fourth year)

If My Dog Could Talk

My dear Jack Russell dog, Mattie Rose, knows all of my deep sorrow. Mattie hears my screams for God to take the suffering away. She licks away my many tears. It's as though my loved one wants to wipe away my tears and can't physically, so she directs Mattie Rose to do it for her. Mattie is ruthless when I'm in deep grief and I can't keep her away. Her tongue laps up my tears and washes my face. I have tried to push her away but she is very strong for a 15 lb dog. I don't like to be licked in the face, but let me tell you, she is on a mission and she won't calm down until all tears are licked away.

I so desperately need to know what my purpose in life is now. God show me my purpose now that I'm not a mother. Mattie still calls me mom. Yes, I can understand doggie language.

Words of encouragement . . .

There is no oil without squeezing the olives, no wine without pressing the grapes, no fragrance without crushing the flowers and no real joy without sorrow.

The Plan Of The Master Weaver

Words of encouragement . . .

"Begin to weave and God will give you the thread."
~German Proverb

It's hard to make sense of a death, but this poem brings me some comfort and understanding. May it ease your pain as you join me in traveling down our path.

Our lives are but fine weavings
That God and we prepare
Each life becomes a fabric planned
And fashioned in His care
We may not always see just how
The weavings intertwine
But we must trust the Master's hand
And follow His design

For He can view the pattern
Upon the upper side
While we must look from underneath
And trust in Him to guide
Sometimes a strand of sorrow
Is added to His plan
And though it's difficult for us
We still must understand
That it's He who fills the shuttle
It's He who knows what's best
So we must weave in patience
And leave to Him the rest
Not till the loom is silent
And the shuttles cease to fly
Shall God unroll the canvas
And explain the reason why
The dark threads are as needed
In the Weaver's skillful hand
As the threads of gold and silver
In the pattern He has planned
~Anonymous~

Stupid Things People May Say

You cannot rely on others to always say the right words and provide the right comfort. Job's "friends" condemned him and did not understand his grief. Job replied: "I have heard many things like these; miserable comforters are you all!" (Job 16:1-2).

People will often try to bring you comfort by making statements that are in reality very hurtful. They offer advice to get you out of your grief. These people have not walked in your shoes. They may not understand the grieving process takes different lengths of time for each person. You must let the grieving process proceed at your own speed, because if you try to rush it, you will only prolong the healing.

~ *Come share my children.*

Children are the greatest gifts we have, and it is nice that you are willing to share. No offense, but seeing what you still have and what I don't does nothing to ease my pain. Your insisting only pushes me farther away from you. Give me time to absorb my loss.

~ *I couldn't live without my child;*
~ *I don't know how you do it.*

Okay, are you trying to tell me that you love your child more than I love mine? Very bluntly, I have two choices: live or kill myself. My faith does not allow me the privilege of suicide and rejoining my Lord and child, so I have to live.

~ *I'm afraid to speak their name.*
~ *I don't want to make you sad.*

My child lived; it doesn't matter how long. Don't be afraid to speak her name and tell stories. Yes, my eyes will most likely tear up, and one may actually break free and slide down my face. It's okay! My heart swells with love and appreciation that you remember. One of my greatest fears is that people will go on living and forget she ever existed.

~ *You can adopt.*

Several people told me this *soon* after the loss. Adoption may be rewarding, but realize that my child was ripped out of my life. There is no replacement.

~ *At least it was only your stepchild.*

A child by blood or child by marriage—what constitutes a real child? A child by marriage is always a child by choice. Please don't attempt to categorize which pain is worse. Stormie and her step-day shared a remarkable loving bond. His pain is deep.

~ *You are doing so well. You are such a strong person.*

What an insensitive remark. Where are you when I'm in the pit of darkness? All I can say is I take each day as it comes. I try to tuck away my shattered soul and continue on with my family and friends.

Some days it works; some days it doesn't.

~ *They are not at the cemetery.*

Thank you for that information. Why, I thought I would just swing on by and gather her up. I go to see her name and the dates of her life spent on earth. The beginning and the ending are carved on that cold slab of rock. It confirms that I am not totally losing my mind. She was here, and she is gone.

~ Time will take care of the pain. It will get easier.

And when did you become father time? It does not matter how much time has passed–days, weeks, months or years. Time passing does not make the pain go away. Don't presume to judge me. You haven't walked in these shoes. I have never done this before, and it is not only unnatural but also very scary. You may take my hand and gently guide me, but don't yank on me, I'm fragile. God made each of His children with different emotions, and we are not on the same timetable.

~ At least you have other children.

Yes, this is a comfort, but each child brings different dynamics to the family. There is a huge gap in the family.

~ Don't worry, she is better off now, she is in a better place.

Yes, my child is in heaven with her Jesus. The troubles and tensions of her earthly existence are behind her; she is safely *home*. This brings me comfort, but I am a mere human, and I want her here with me. Call it being selfish–I don't care.

~ You'll see her again someday.

Someday does not bring me comfort. I desperately need to see, feel, touch, hear, and smell my child now. The Bible leaves no doubt that there is life after death. The Bible tells me there is a time to live and a time to die. I don't know how long I have on this earth, and I am very impatient. My heart's desire is to see her now.

~ God needed another angel in heaven.

God has enough angels in heaven. He didn't need mine. I refuse to believe my Father would intentionally make me suffer this horrible loss. It's so difficult to make sense of a life cut short; maybe she had spent her allotted time on earth–it was her time.

~ It's been such a long time ago.
~ It's time to move on.
~ Get over it.

Again with the time thing. I will *always* feel the pain. She was a major part of me. I will move on at my own pace. Some stay in the pit of darkness the remainder of their lives. Quit rushing me!

Words of encouragement . . .

"Kind words can be short and easy to speak,
but their echoes are truly endless."
~ Mother Teresa

Helpful Hints For Dealing With Grieving Parents

Words of encouragement . . .

Prayers are bandages on a healing heart.

~ *Have true compassion.*

Sometimes people get caught up in Sunday school, choir rehearsals, and who's sitting in the church pews; they lose sight of the needs of those around them. They are compassionate Christians and truly feel sorry for those who are hurting, but sympathetic thoughts are not true compassion. True compassion is very personal and close to the heart. True compassion is active involvement that expresses God's merciful heart in words and deeds.

~ *Don't wear you feelings on your shirtsleeves.*

Don't take anything personal or be judgmental. Don't make this about your needs or feelings. We are trying to survive.

~ The pain is still there even though several years have passed.

It will always affect us. The person you knew before is gone! Please don't be afraid to get close to the *new* person. We still need compassion and human contact.

~ Send cards at random times.

Mail cards or notes of remembrance, sympathy, loss, pain and suffering or just to say hello. You don't have to remember exact dates. When you think of the loss, call or send a short note. Let us know when you are thinking of us. It is very comforting to open the mailbox and find a note. Share a story or event you remember about our loved one. Who knows, we may need uplifted at that exact moment.

~ I can't say it enough times: It is okay if our eyes tear up, and one happens to escape down our faces.

Sometimes the tears are full of pain, and sometimes the tears are full of bittersweet joy, but most of all, the tears are healing. They let some of the bottled up emotions out.

~ As parents, we are programmed to protect our children; did we fail at out most important job?

There are times so many different emotions are bolting through our bodies that we don't have a clue what to do.

~ Lots of hugs. We need to be comforted with touch.

We miss holding our loved one. A simple touch can send a message that words cannot describe.

~ Phone calls, even if all you hear are our tears.

It's okay; you are doing a good thing! Calls anytime are welcomed, but remember to call on dates that are important to us; the loved one's birthday and date of death will always be difficult for us. We need to know that our loved one has not been forgotten. Remember a tremendous fear is after time passes our child will fade away from memories.

~ *Start sentences with, I choose to believe.*

For instance, *I choose to believe* that our loved ones are always with us. *I choose to believe* does not tell us what we should be thinking or feeling. It says what you believe and it could be helpful to shine a different light on the loss.

~ *Send emails, even though you don't always get a reply.*

They remind us you are thinking of us, and you don't have to be intimidated by our tears. Although, remember, tears are not bad things. They are God's way of cleansing the tattered soul.

~ *Bring food.*

Don't forget us after the first couple of weeks. It takes a long time to be able to concentration enough to cook, not to mention grocery shop. Nourishment is important. It takes a lot of fuel to grieve.

~ *"No" at this time doesn't always mean no.*

We are so confused and lost. Don't be overly pushy, but don't quit trying on the first no and don't get your feelings hurt if we keep saying no. This is a new life and we don't know how to live it yet.

~ *HAVE PATIENCE!*

Simply . . . Very gently take our hand and walk *with* us through this journey called life.

Words of encouragement . . .

Out of all the treasures in the world there is nothing more precious than giving someone a piece of your heart.

God's Prescription For Healing

There is no short cut to heal from grief; you must go through it, not around it. Each step you take is an important part of your healing. Remember *Foot Prints in the Sand:* Why has God forsaken you? Why was there only one set of footprints, not two–his and yours? Because He carried you! You may not feel His presence at this time in your grief journey. Don't be alarmed; you are still in a state of non-functioning. He is carrying you through to your healing.

I've had enough Lord!
(1 King 19:4)

If I'll just follow the Lord's prescriptions for discouragement, given here to Elijah, I should be able to regain control of my emotions and myself:

1. Get enough rest (1 Kings 19:5)
Grieving is very tiresome–it drains energy.

2. Eat healthy foods on a regular basis (1 Kings 19:6)
Half a chocolate cake does not a healthy meal make. Foods

high in protein and low in sugar will give you strength your body needs to grieve. I'm still experimenting, but there may be a connection to my clothes shrinking and chocolate.

3. Spend some quiet time with yourself and the Lord (1 Kings 19:12)
There's no dodging it. No matter how difficult it is to concentrate, spending some alone time with your Lord will help provide the stability to find your bearings.

4. Now go! (1 Kings 19:15)
Keep your mind, body and soul in motion. Stand up and walk. You must not let yourself stay immobilized.

If you can make rules 1–3 your priorities, number 4 will usually follow.

Words of encouragement . . .

We don't change God's message
—His message changes us.

How To Survive First Year

Words of encouragement . . .

When the storm seems unbearable.
There is always a hand to grab you.
Wings to wrap you,
And a love to warm you.

~ Keep Moving - If you stop you may get stuck and never move again.

It was so difficult, but I returned to work the week after my daughter's death. My co-workers were wonderful. They were not my family who tried to fix me. They just surrounded me with support and kept me supplied with chocolate. I was not able to think clearly. It was as though I was running in warped time–underwater. I worked as a senior secretary in a high-paced company, and multi-tasking was my specialty. My mind just shut down and it was as though I was a foreigner in my own skin. My body shook all the time. Stormie and I were so connected a part of my spirit and soul died with her.

~ *Grieve - Give yourself permission to grieve.*

You may feel overwhelmed, but feel the pain and emotions that are uniquely yours. People who have not walked in your shoes may try to instruct you as to the "stages" in grieving. Let them speak, but don't allow their lack of wisdom to impact your karma. God knows what you need, and He is guiding you even if you cannot feel Him. Be assured that His peace is always there waiting for you. Right now it may seem that God has left you. He doesn't hear your cries. But God sent his only son to die for our sins. *His only son.* What an awesome, selfless God we have. Someday you will feel Him again. Sit still and believe in His promises and rest in His peace.

"Now may the Lord of peace himself give you peace at all times and in every way. The Lord be with all of you." (2 Thessalonians 3:16)

~ *Grab your pillow and close your doors.*

My life-saving grief guide taught me this. Set an alarm for 10 minutes. Beat your pillow with your fist and scream out "why did you leave me" and keep on hitting and screaming and emotions will come out that you don't even know are inside you. Ten minutes is a *long* time. If you are exhausted before the timer goes off, it's okay. Remember, you are not on a timetable in your grief journey. Word of advice, you may not want to do this with a feather pillow.

~ Talk

You may feel it is useless to talk about your grief because no one truly understands what you are going through. You're speaking a foreign language and there's no way anybody can know what you're feeling. There is absolutely no way anyone can know the depth of your pain. But I do.

Search for a person that is not judgmental. It may take a few misses, but you will know when you've found the person that clicks with you. It likely will be someone that is not close to you, and that is a good thing. Our loved ones tend to try to fix us, and that is an impossible task. A problem can be fixed; but we are living a situation, and situations cannot be changed.

A friend connected me with an email mom in the first months of my loss. Her son, Ben, was killed a few months before my daughter. She has read my most despairing thoughts. I am encouraging you, actually giving you permission, to say exactly what just wants to come out. I can't stress enough you must set your grief free. Don't keep shoving it down deep inside.

~ Doctor's care - be very careful of any doctor's care you seek.

I was very cautious of medications at first. The day my child died, the emergency room doctor wanted to sedate me. I would not allow any medications that were going to make me go to sleep. I needed to feel my pain. As the first year of her death passed, I was injured in a freak accident at a home improvement store. My neck, shoulders, arms and hands were and will forever be in constant pain. After undergoing two shoulder surgeries, I was referred to pain management doctors. I lost my job and eventually was declared totally disabled. I was put on heavy medication in the name of pain management. I became more and more depressed. I sought treatment with the only psychiatrist that my insurance covered. The first visit scheduled for 1½ hours lasted a mere 15 minutes. He started me on medication for depression and sleep aids. Every visit I found myself deeper in depression and he would add another medication. I knew I was dying a slow death.

How I Survived Years Two, Three And Four

Years two and three came and went. I don't remember a lot, just depression and no hope for life. My family and friends kept telling me they were seeing me die before their eyes. I continued on with the pain management medications, which kept me knocked down. I was in great physical pain and depended on medical doctors for guidance. I searched in vain for doctors that would assist me in backing off some of the medication, but eventually lost all hope and I slowly retreated to a dark hole.

After four years of gut-retching sorrow, Jesus knew when I could withstand the realization that I had to first face my grief, and then relocate it or die. Through a web of friends and Jesus' guidance, I was connected with a wonderful grief counselor who guided me through my emotions.

Finally I made it out the stormy doors of hell, and in the doors to rainbow hope.

My Journey Through The Storm to Find Rainbows

I continued to seek other physicians' help, trying to get off of some of the heavy medication, only to find them placing me on more. Jesus finally led me to a wonderful physiatrist, who, after reading my list of medications, told me point blank that I could drop dead with my next breathe. I chose to admit myself to a hospital. It was scary walking through a new set of stormy doors. I was the only person on the detox floor that was not a repeat customer. I told them up front that my mind was not addicted to the medications, it was my body. As you can imagine, they had a chuckle under their breath. After days of pure physical hell, the addictive medications worked out of my system. However, my grief was still strong. The staff agreed that my mind was not addicted. After one, two, three, four, five, six, seven long days, I walked out the doors to rainbow hope.

While in the hospital, I realized my will to live was lost from the moment I received the phone call of my child's accident. I called Stormie's father and asked him to bring her journals to the hospital. I was grasping at straws to try to find the desire to live. He had promised me from her death to share her written words, but they were empty promises. He came, but didn't bring her journals. Instead he brought her backpack, which is priceless to all of us. She carried the backpack through all her church missions, schools, and travels with family and friends. As you can imagine, it was a little tattered and torn, but it showed the true spirit of Storm. It was covered with a selection of patches that mirrored her travels and her interests. I was so touched that he actually came. Little did I know how the visit would end.

We shared precious memories of our daughter. He told me that he sought my forgiveness for all the past hurtful things he put me through. I gave him my forgiveness, but later had a war with myself to keep my word.

I asked him to lend me Storm's backpack until I was released from the hospital. I had chosen to hand the backpack over to Stormie's' stepmother four years earlier when we were dividing up her belongings. It broke my heart to let it go, but holding true to Storm's memory, I was trying to be a true Christian.

I sat before him on my knees on the hospital floor that day, pleading with my soul and sanity to lend me her backpack. He not only told me no, he never shed an ounce of compassion. I never felt the touch of his hand or any care for my broken soul.

I have read in the Bible to be aware that Jesus could come as a homeless man, a small child, etc. How did he know in his heart that Jesus was not on that floor with me, inside my soul as I begged through sobs of my shattered soul, grieving the loss of my baby girl, crying out for his compassion? I wonder how Stormie Lynn would have felt seeing her mother begging her father for something that would bring her comfort for the last three days in the hospital.

June 11, 2005 he left Baylor Hospital with me laying in bed, in a fetal position. As I lay there suffering, I felt the hand of Jesus lift me and wipe away my tears. From that moment on, Christ gave me a desire to learn to live again.

Words of encouragement . . .

"You can clutch the past so tightly to your chest, that it leaves your arms too full to embrace the present."
~Jan Glidewell

Mother's And Father's Day

Tim and I didn't celebrate Mother's and Father's Day. We felt like we no longer had a child, so the holidays didn't exist for us.

Words of encouragement . . .

The point of power is
always in the present moment.

Father's Day Gift

I *choose to believe* Stormie spoke to me and I'd like to share a condensed version of the letter to my husband Timothy on June 17, 2005.

"Today I sit here at this very moment to share with you the words that keep going on and on in my mind. I realize that once a mother always a mother and once a father always a father. When a parent passes to the other side they don't ever stop being a parent.

I guess what I am trying to say is *we* still are Storm's parents. I need to be remembered on Mother's Day, and you deserve to be remembered as well on Father's Day. I think from this day forward we need to do something special on those days so we always hear and feel her love even greater. We don't have to die everyday, but live happily and love to each other just like she showed us.

Oh my goodness, she loved you so very much. She gave her mother to you. She told me, as we sat in the middle of the bed sharing our most intimate beliefs, "You will be okay now, Mom, you have Tim." God works in mysteries ways. This was less than one month before her death–it was as though things in her life were falling into place.

I pray you allow yourself to shed your tears and smile through those tears as you remember her love for you. You were so very, very important in her life.

> She wants you to sit back and relax and hear her.
> She is saying, 'Hi, Tim, what's happening?'
> Can't you just hear her bubbly voice?"

Mother's Day Gift

May 9, 2004

I told my family I was skipping Mother's Day, and I almost did. It had been three years since Stormie's death, and I tried to convince myself that I should be able to move on. I took a rose to her gravesite. I sat and cried that I missed her touch so deeply. I cried myself out and returned home.

I was emptying the vacuum off the back deck when I saw a butterfly. Stormie and I always enjoyed butterflies. I kept on with my task and saw the butterfly land on the post to my left. All of a sudden the butterfly came down and touched my right arm.

I was amazed and a little skeptical of what had really happened. Wow, the butterfly flew down, touched my arm again, and returned back to the post. She lightly kissed my arm three times. I went in the house to tell Timothy and he responded, "Well, I guess, you just got your Mother's day gift."

Later I took Tim outside to show him where the butterfly had been, and much to my surprise, she was still there. She fluttered right down and kissed my arm again!

Words of encouragement . . .

No heart could be
happier
than the heart that
believes in
angels.

When All Hope Seems Lost

When I lost hope for those years, my life was a blur. My body went through the motions, but my mind just couldn't get there. It was like being in a raging river with the water rising and I was slowly drowning. Have you ever gotten water up your nose? Remember the raw burning pain? My pain burned and was raw.

I can close my eyes and see her playing with her dog, Friend, that my brother gave her when she was just a few years old. I remember the day she watched her first drama movie Lassie Come Home, and she cried uncontrollably worried that Lassie would never find her way home. I can now relate to the helpless feeling of being lost and the difficult journey finding my way home. She tried to change Friend's name to Lassie and was upset when Friend wouldn't come when she called the new name. I told her to name her Friend Lassie and suddenly everything was right in her small world again. If only it was that simple and easy to make everything right in my small world.

Recap Of Tips On Learning To Live Again

Words of encouragement . . .
"In silence He listens to us,
In silence He speaks to our souls.
Take some time out to be silent with Him."
~Mother Teresa

Get quite and remember

~ Get quite and close your eyes and remember their voice.

~ Practice picturing their face in your mind so when you miss them the most, you can close your eyes and instantly see their face and hear their voice.

~ If you can't think clearly, it's okay, just feel your body breathing in and out.

Nourishment

~ Grief burns a lot of energy.

~ Eat healthy-but a little chocolate is acceptable.

Move

~ If you sit still you may get stuck.

~ Keep moving, even if you are going in circles.

~ Don't give up if you trip and fall; get up, brush off, and move again.

Don't over medicate

~ Feel your feelings all the way.

~ Some drugs may ease the immediate pain, but sooner or later you have to deal with the grief. Time does not make it any less painful, but go on your own timetable.

~ Cry until you can't cry anymore, and then cry some more.

~ Tears are God's way of cleansing the soul.

~ Crying is very tiring and it may help you to sleep.

Talk

~ Tell stories about your child, they lived.

~ Celebrate their life.

~ Mourn their death.

~ Express your emotions.

~ Share your grief-Reach out to other mothers who are walking in your shoes. It is so healing to share with someone who knows how you feel and doesn't judge you.

Special Mementos

~ Hold on to items that bring them closer to you-material items that you can physically touch.

~ Make a memory wall and fill it full of pictures that make you smile.

Write I *remembers*

~ I remember her coming home from college and lying in the yard spread eagle looking up to the heavens. Taking a deep breath and saying she was finally home..

~ *I remember the first day of kindergarten. I thought she would need me to comfort her, but Miss Independence pushed me out the door. I confess I did shed a few tears.*

Find Joy

~ *Focus on something that you see at random that reminds you of your child. For instance, when I see a butterfly, I think of Stormie sending me kisses. When I see a blue bird or red bird I can hear her voice, "Hi, Little Mama, what's happening?"*

~ *When I sleep on her pillow, I can imagine her special smell.*

Focus on something positive that you can control

~ *You have no control over the death and*

feel so helpless–In the beginning months I focused on the hazardous intersection where the accident occurred. It was an intersection of two state highways where weekly accidents occurred. I wanted different safety precautions put in place. The state highway department told me that it would never happen. I had several prayer visits with God and within one year the intersection was complete reworked. Don't think it wasn't a difficult task. But with Stormie's former connections with two state representatives (she interned in Washington DC with them), many letters from her professors, and pictures, letters and visits from me, it was accomplished. What can I say; I was a pain in the butt mother that wouldn't take no for an answer. God is so good.

Holidays

~ *Remember the true meaning.*

~ *Mix them up.*

~ *Go to completely different places.*

~ *Share gifts.*

~ *Celebrate them don't hide away.*

~ *Start new traditions.*

~ *Give yourself permission to grieve for the life that is no longer.*

Make a list of what you miss the most, what you feel you have lost. Keep a piece of paper handy and keep adding to the list until you are empty. Use the list below as a starting point.

Miss the most:

- ~ *Your friend*
- ~ *Their smile*
- ~ *Being needed*
- ~ *Being a mom*

Have lost:

- ~ *Your encourager*
- ~ *Your pride and joy*
- ~ *Your source of delight*

Read the list out loud speaking and explain each until you run out of words to say. God knows your deepest needs, and He alone can provide. It's important that you don't omit this step.

"And my God will meet all your needs according to his glorious riches in Christ Jesus." (Philippians 4:19)

Find your power

This is one of the most important advices I can offer. Without your power, you have no strength. Without strength, you can't go on living. Living can make you very weak. You must find a different direction in life and allow yourself to live the different life. The old one is no more. Relocate it and tuck it away. It will sneak out on occasions and that's okay. Just don't let it stay long. Set a deadline, for instance a day or week, then no matter how down you feel, get up and move on.

Grieving mothers are everywhere and you never know what one small outreach can mean to another.

Tears happen. Endure, grieve and move on. The only person who is with us our entire life is ourselves. My daddy always told me that you make your own happiness each day.

Surround yourself with what you love.

~ I now like to work in the yard.

~ I like the color pink.

~ I want fresh flowers in the house.

~ I started sewing quilts and painted the Bungalow's sewing room with lime green stripes. I filled it with items of Stormie that make me smile: framed cards, gifts and her first doll she named Baby Schott.

~ Find whatever brings you joy, whether it's a pet, keepsakes, music-whatever. Your home is your refuge. You and I didn't have a choice to begin all over, but we do have a choice to begin brand new.

Live fully while you are alive.

~ My husband and I have a new life now, and we look at it as an adventure.

~ I choose to believe that my child is in heaven watching me. How can she be happy if all she sees is her mom with a shattered soul? For her sake, as well as for mine, I must find peace and not just survive, but live my life fully here on earth.

~ Don't be afraid to try something different. Who knows, lime green may be your color, too!

Words of encouragement . . .

A joyful heart is good medicine.
It heals the body when it's down and
lifts the spirit from within.

Find your Happy Place

She was sweeter than the chocolate chip cookie dough we used to share while watching a chick flick. Was it tears of love that welled up in my eyes, or did her squinty-eyed smile actually sparkle in the light? I can close my eyes and see the scar that went through her right eyebrow that was the result of her jumping on the bed when she was three. I can close my eyes and hear her sweet voice calling to me, "MoMe."

I discovered I could go to my happy place. How can you find your happy place? Well let's go there together. Close your eyes. Now, think of the happiest memory of your young child. Remember the fun you had doing silly things together that only you and your child could appreciate?

I think I can see you smiling! You must have found your happy place.

Many of us crucify ourselves between two thieves–regret for the past and fear of the future. After four years, I am living in my own happy place. At least I'm there most of the time. When I find myself getting down, I only allow it to get to me for a short period of time, then I find my happy place and smile.

A moment of pure happiness will last you a lifetime in a memory. Give yourself permission to tuck away the bad times that you cannot change and feel the joy your child brought you so many times. May Jesus bless you with the ability to find your happy place.

The Most Important Conversations Are The Ones You Have With Yourself

You are the only person that has spent every moment with you, and you are your most important critic. There is no opinion so vitally important to your well being as the opinion you have of yourself, and this very moment you may not be thinking very positive thoughts. As you read this, you're having a conversation with yourself and may not be even aware that you are doing it. We all have a running commentary in our heads on events and our reactions to them.

We must be aware of the silent conversations we have with ourselves. Are you nurturing to yourself? Often we are our own worst critic. Do you ever give yourself a pat on the back for the strength that you have? You've traveled down a path that some get lost on and *never* reach home.

Don't always look at the walk ahead as being dark and lonely, but instead think positive thoughts.

There is scientific proof that our mind and heath are connected. The mind is a mysterious organ.

We cannot process emotions we can't feel. Therefore, we must dig deep down to all the emotions we didn't have the strength to process early on in our grief. It's frightening, but no matter how uncomfortable or hurtful, we must call on them to surface. The best advice for working with emotions is not to try to understand them. Remind yourself that emotions are irrational. Our emotional self-conversations remind us of all the negative things we've done. Example of irrational emotions: if we had been a better parent, bad things would not have happened to our child–everything negative in their life was our fault. If emotions were rational, they wouldn't be emotions, they would be thoughts. Thoughts are rational, and problem solving oriented. They demand explanation, understanding and solutions.

Unlike thoughts, emotions don't need explanations, to be understood, or have solutions; but they do need to be acknowledged. Once emotions are felt, they live in the present. Again that time thing: it doesn't matter how long ago things happened; you still feel the same way about it right now. Trying to explain or justifying feelings is nothing but an attempt to question reality. It is important to get quiet with yourself, get in touch with your emotions and turn your thoughts off. The more you think, the less you feel.

We reach a time in our healing journey that we must quit denying the feelings that are within us and call them to surface. I know how deeply it hurts. To those who haven't walked our path, this may sound easy; but in reality, it is very, very difficult. It takes time to go here and keep in mind that we are all on different timetables. We often use our thinking to prevent ourselves from feeling in ways that allow us to process our emotions correctly. Just the same way we might have problems with digesting food, we also suffer from emotional indigestion. But there is not magic pill to make us feel comfortable. We must feel it fully, and then tuck it away. As I've said before, face them, relocate them and don't allow yourself to pull them out of relocation often.

I choose to tell myself that today I will not have negative thoughts or feelings, but will find some joy. I get quiet, close my eyes and take myself to happier times and relive the peace and joy. Give yourself permission to smile, even if for a short period. The more often you have positive conversations with yourself, the easier it is to automatically control your feelings.

I won't lie to you and tell you this works every time, but I will take joy any day rather than the dark hole of grief.

Words of encouragement . . .

Happiness depends
on
happenings,
but
joy depends on
Christ.

I've Learned

~ ***I've learned*** . . . That we should be glad God doesn't answer all of our prayers

~ ***I've learned*** . . . That the Lord didn't do it all in one day, so take each day as it comes.

~ ***I've learned*** . . . That life is like a piece of fudge. The closer to the end, the faster it goes.

~ ***I've learned*** . . . That it's those small things that make the best memories in life.

~ ***I've learned*** . . . People are like tea bags- you have to put them in hot water before you know how strong they are.

~ ***I've learned*** . . . Love begins with a smile, grows with a kiss and ends with a tear.

Stories Of Hope And Journaling

"The best and most beautiful things in the world cannot be seen or even touched. They must be felt with the heart. "
~Helen Keller

I *choose to believe* that when we cross over, we shed our human shell and the spirit lives forever. The stories to follow are proof enough for me.

Conversation with Kim

On Friday, January 04, 2002, I sat at my daughter's graveside remembering just a few days earlier an agreement I made with my dear friend Kim on her deathbed–she would hug my daughter Stormie in heaven and I in return would be here on earth for her young daughter Kaylie.

Describing to me what she saw, Kim said, "It's like looking through a window from heaven to earth. You can see a person with their entire life trailing with them like an airplane leaves its mark in the sky trailing behind it. Our lives do the same thing. The colors are so beautiful."

Granny's Story

On July 11, 1996, my sweet Granny went home to Jesus. She had been in a semi-coma for 24 hours. My mother walked in the room, and Granny spoke her last words, "You be a good girl. It is so beautiful there, so very beautiful!"

Words of encouragement . . .

A happier heart cannot be found, than the heart that believes in angels!

I remember . . .

Within a few weeks of Storm's crossing over, a live oak tree was planted at her gravesite. I went everyday to see her name etched into the granite headstone to remind me she was gone. One day, I noticed a bird nest was on a lower limb of the freshly planted tree. Three eggs were there. As time passed, I watched the little mama bird sitting on the nest, the birds hatching and growing; and one day, just as quickly as they were there, they were gone.

As the first year came, a second nest appeared in an unlikely place at our home in Denton. Stormie often gave Tim items for cooking on the grill. One year she gave him a funny apron and chef's hat. The apron hangs on a nail by our back door that we use daily. As a matter of fact, at that time we kept a spare key to our house in the apron pocket. One day, I went to reach into the pocket for the key and saw a bird nest with six eggs. That little mama bird would sit on her nest and watch us as we went by. Sometimes, she would fly frantically around in a circle, and back into the pocket she would go. Six baby birds hatched. They chirped so much I thought they were hungry and worried their mama had abandoned them. She hadn't. One day, just as quickly as they were there, they were gone.

Slowly the second year came, and yes, once again a bird nest appeared, this time at our Bungalow at Lake Texoma. I uncovered the grill, and there, in the mitten that Stormie gave Tim, was a nest with eggs. The little mama bird would fly off when we uncovered the grill and would return when we finished cooking. As usual, there were baby birds and just as quickly as they were there, they were gone.

The third year came, and the bird nest was back in Denton, once again on the back deck, beside the back door that we use daily. This time it was in a storage crate that sat on a table. The nest was under some boxes, so I couldn't see it as clearly as the others. But baby birds hatched; and once again, just as quickly as they were there, they were gone.

Now the fourth year came, and once again in the pocket of the apron appeared a little mama bird. She had just begun to make her nest when I reached inside to retrieve the house key. She flew out and scared the bejeepies out of me. She abandoned that nest and set up a new one high on a beam under the carport. Needless to say, this time I could not see into the nest. But when those little babies hatched, they stuck their heads out so we could talk. Just as quickly as they were there, they were gone.

The fifth year has yet to come, and I eagerly wait to see where a nest will appear.

My Journal: April 18, 2001

I remember when I had my back surgery in the mid 1980's; I had, for lack of a better description, an out-of-body experience. After being discharged, I got an infection and had to be readmitted to the hospital in Dallas. I was at Baylor Hospital in Dallas alone for about three days. With the combination of pain and loneliness, I thought I was useless to all and wanted to drift away. I quit eating and answering my phone.

I found myself zooming up from the bed into space. It took my stomach away like if you suddenly dropped. I instantly felt no pain, there was sunshine all around me and I felt an overwhelming release. I told myself, "This is all right–I think I'll stay right here." Then I heard Stormie's voice calling to me, "MoMe, please don't go. Don't leave me. I need you. MoMe, please don't go." I thought just for a split second about staying where I was, but I couldn't bear hearing my sweet child crying out to me. I came back into my body.

I lay there for a short while with no pain. I actually walked to the bathroom and back to bed with no pain. Prior to that I was using a bedpan. Slowly the pain came back and I found myself alone in the room again.

I *choose to believe* that Stormie is in that place I visited such a long time ago. Even though I was only there for a short period, I can remember the beautiful colors and the peace I felt. I *choose to believe* God allowed me that visit so I would know what a marvelous place she is in.

My Journal: August 10, 2001 9:13 am

Stormie, tomorrow will be your fifth month with the angels. It seems like years, and then again like you should be walking in the door, or calling on the phone any moment. I want to hear your voice.

I feel your presence with me all the time. I *choose to believe* that I will see you on the other side. I wish so often that my life would end now, but then it would be so hard on Maw Maw, Papaw, and Timothy. I'm torn between my selfish needs and theirs.

I thank God everyday that you were with me for 23 years. I always told you and meant it from the bottom of my soul, that you are the best thing I've done on earth. It was wonderful being pregnant, having you grow inside me and feeling you move. I wanted to be with you when you experienced the same.

I miss you and I love you so very much. Please stay with me always.

Love, Mama

My Journal: October 29, 2003

I am so very broken hearted. Kandice's wedding was Saturday and all I could see was you, Storm. It should have been you I was watching. It should have been you smiling with Scott. It should have been you with all your friends and family. It should have been you.

I feel like I'm in a tunnel with nowhere to go. Just darkness. It takes such an effort to walk, talk, etc. I feel like I did after you died. I am sick to my stomach. My heart is crying blood tears. I don't know how much more of this I can endure.

Words of encouragement . . .

There are moments in life when you
miss someone so much that you just
want to pick them from your dreams and
hug them for real!

I Bid You Farewell

I close with a verse from the Bible that to me says it all:

There is a time for everything, and a season for every activity under heaven.

A time to be born and a time to die
A time to plant and a time to uproot
A time to kill and a time to heal
A time to tear down and a time to refrain
A time to weep and a time to laugh
A time to mourn and a time to dance
A time to scatter stones and a time to gather them
A time to embrace and a time to refrain
A time to search and a time to give up
A time to keep and a time to throw away
A time to tear and a time to mend
A time to be silent and a time to speak
A time to love and a time to hate
A time for war and a time for peace
(Ecclesiastes 3: 2–8)

My Stormie loved to laugh and dance.

I can close my eyes and *hear her laughter* and *see her dancing* in a beautiful field of wildflowers.

Each time you hear a waterfall or watch a humming bird fly, or you see a field of wildflower or a rainbow after the storm, it's all God whispering, "This is Me."

May you catch heaven's rays . . .
Stormie's Little Mama, Sherry

Contact author Sherry Boyd Neu
or order more copies of this book at

TATE PUBLISHING, LLC

127 East Trade Center Terrace
Mustang, Oklahoma 73064

(888) 361 - 9473

Tate Publishing, LLC

www.tatepublishing.com